Volu

of the series

The Last Word
on the Parsha

Shlomo Schwartz

The Last Word on *VaYikra*
Book of Leviticus

Shlomo Schwartz

An examination of the often overlooked last words of the parsha. Do they just tidy up loose ends or do they constitute the final objective?

First Edition March 2018

Notice to Reader: I sometimes use phrases such as "this doesn't make sense" or "outrageous claim" and the like in reference to a Torah verse or commentary. Some readers have taken offense to such phrases, viewing them as disrespectful to the Torah. To them I proclaim my passion that Torah messages resonate within us. Because of that passion, when I encounter some piece of Torah that does not resonate with my world, as I understand and experience it, I first react expressively, as above. Since the Torah has to make sense and cannot be outrageous or the like, this then motivates me to analytically discover how to reconcile my world with the Torah. If that passion were missing, I would probably do the common thing and accept any answer that deflects the problem. To my thinking, that would constitute a lack of respect for the Torah and what it has to offer me.

Foreword

I have used the translations and transliterations introduced by Artscroll with one determined exception. When translating the holy name *Elohim*, **I have used "Lord" rather than Artscroll's "God"**. I feel "God" is a gross error because, when that word is written with an uppercase "G", every English reader immediately identifies it with the single Creator of the universe. However, *Elohim* is often written with suffixes, such as *Eloheinu,* in which case it is translated as "our God". The possessive implies that there are other Creator Gods who are not ours. Even though most readers will immediately realize that this is patently false, nevertheless, it is misleading. I have heard people say of others, "their God is not my God" thus suggesting that there is more than one Creator God, *chaleela*. The very statement alone is blasphemous. What they should say is, **"their understanding of God is faulty"**. If they did, it might lead to a much more productive discussion which, after all, should be the end goal of every translation.

Another example that causes confusion is *"elohim acheirim"* translated as "other gods" or "gods of others" by Artscroll, using a lowercase "g". In this case, the translation itself is not misleading but it is inconsistent with the way the same word, *elohim*, is translated in other contexts.

Translating *Elohim* with "Lord" solves all these problems. There are other Lords, even ones with uppercase "L" such as those in the House of Lords of the United Kingdom. "Lord" implies "boss", the one who is in charge and orders things, which is exactly what the halacha suggests we mean and think of when using this holy name.

Another departure I make from Artscroll relates to the holiest of the seven holy names of God. When translating the four letter name that Artscroll "translates" as Hashem, I sometimes use "Infinite" or "Eternal" because I feel these terms more accurately convey the surface meaning of the word which seems to be a composition of "He was, He is, He will be", i.e. **Hashem is eternal and, therefore, infinite**.

When discussing other Hebrew phrases, I will often transliterate the Hebrew in italics, insert a "/", and follow with my own translation in non-italics. When there is more than one word in the Hebrew, English or both, I connect the words with a "-" so that **the reader's eye can easily discern** where the translation stops. Even for well known Hebrew words, I want to be sure to at least once mention an English version of the phrase because that is what will register most meaningfully on the mind of English readers.

In contrast, I have used regular typeface to reference the Hebrew names or acronyms of Rabbis and book titles and have not bothered to compile a bibliography out of respect for Google who will provide all such information more accurately and comprehensively than I would.

I debated internally whether to standardize on *yeshivish* pronunciations such as ***Shabbos*** or on ***Shabbat****,* the modern Hebrew version. The former is more native to me while the latter is, I think, more dominant. In the end, I decided not to standardize in the belief that both will survive the culture wars; it will be like the two ways of pronouncing tomato, with the hard or soft "a".

Also for the reader's eye, I highlight certain phrases with bold typeface to facilitate referencing back to an earlier key point.

Table of Contents

Parsha 1: Hashem Calls Everyone   11

Parsha 2: Command Performance   21

Parsha 3: Becoming Holy   29

Parsha 4: Understanding Tzaraas Today   37

Parsha 5: Why Loshon Hora is the Worst Sin   45

Parsha 6: Recovering From Stumbling   53

Parsha 7: Is That Old Time Magic Still Here?   61

Parsha 8: Seize the Day, Don't Curse It   67

Parsha 9: Seen Hashem Lately?   73

Parsha 10: Received at Sinai   83

ויקרא – VaYikra

He Called

21 Masoretic Paragraphs, 111 verses;
Leviticus Chapters 1 – 5

Parsha 1: Hashem Calls Everyone

The last verse of ויקרא shocked me but that turned out to be a good thing because it led me to **discover a hidden message that unfolds over the course of the parsha**. I was shocked because, of all the characters described in the parsha, this last one is surely the guiltiest of all, yet was treated the lightest. The parsha had been describing sinners of various types, all of whom had sinned but, because the sins had been accidental, each could gain forgiveness through a sacrificial offering designed especially for that sin. Once the sacrificial offering has been brought, the text assures each of the accidental sinners *v'nislach lo* "it will be forgiven".

However, the last person described is not an accidental sinner. He has acted wilfully by first robbing and then swearing falsely. This kind of criminal behavior should make him a social outcast. Nevertheless, after bringing his particular sacrificial offering, the last verse not only promises the standard "it will be forgiven" but also incredulously grants him a blanket pardon, "for any of all the things he might do to incur guilt". This is much more extensive than the forgiveness granted everyone else in the parsha who acted in error. **It just doesn't seem fair!** It also doesn't seem prudent - we ought to make an example of such people.

I kept stepping back through the parsha looking for an answer without success until I reached the beginning. That is when I started to **appreciate how the parsha unfolds its message**, first with voluntary offerings then with mandatory ones. The first eleven of the twenty-one paragraphs of ויקרא (Lev. Ch.1–3) introduce the three voluntary offerings of *Olah*/Elevation, *Mincha*/Gift and *Shlomim*/Peace. These offerings are ones we volunteer to bring to the Sanctuary any time the spirit moves us to do so. Thus, more than half of this parsha's paragraphs describe the relationship we have with Hashem as one of easy access. I find this evocative of the relationship young children have with their parents. Just like children feel free to grab hold of, jump onto, or barge in on parents whenever they want, so too every Jew is free to call upon his Maker and connect with the Infinite without appointment.

This, in turn, reminds me that children grow up and eventually break away from parents. Often they exercise their independence by making their own decisions without consultation. Frequently, **such decisions lead to embarrassing results with a social cost too exorbitant for the young offender to bear.** When this happens, the wise parent or mentor will be ready with a "make-it-right" plan that offers a more affordable "payment" for the crime. This allows the young offender to re-enter society and again make independent decisions, confident they can recover from inevitable mistakes in the future. The rest of the parsha may very well be describing how Hashem provides us with a similar recovery plan.

The last ten paragraphs (Lev. Ch. 4-5) describe various types of *Chatas*/Sin and *Asham*/Guilt offerings. These differ from the offerings in the first eleven paragraphs in that they are not voluntary. *Chatas* and *Asham* offerings become mandatory when someone commits a grievous sin in error or under mitigating circumstances. (Wilful sins cannot be atoned with an offering; they are treated differently as discussed elsewhere in the Torah.) When a person inadvertently commits a grievous sin, that person is likely to experience extreme guilt and embarrassment from having been involved in such socially unacceptable deeds. To recover from such effects, **Hashem provides an affordable "make-it-right" plan to "pay" for the error** - the duty to bring an offering.

Almost without exception, these make-it-right plans end with the uplifting promise, *v'nislach lo* "it will be forgiven him" - **he can recover.** These words assuring forgiveness are repeated in a regular pattern right up to the end of the parsha. However, the last two paragraphs introduce changes to that pattern that fairly shout for our attention. Before addressing that shout out, I think it useful to replicate the buildup that the parsha employs to unfold its message by dwelling on some of the interim steps. For the reader who wishes to skip ahead to "quiet the shouting", I have provided a marker point up ahead with the heading of <u>The Last Two Paragraphs</u>.

The first of these make-it-right plans is provided for the *Chatas*/Sin of a *Kohen-Gadol*/High-Priest who erred in judgment. This is the only paragraph (Lev. 4:1-12) that does not mention the promise "it will be forgiven him". Perhaps, no forgiveness was necessary because his error was an inadvertent misinterpretation of the law, not arising from glaring ignorance. In other *Chatas*/Sin cases, the error arose from some carelessness. But here, **what was the *Kohen Gadol* to do?** He was in the middle of a service, one probably only he was authorized to do and thought he was performing correctly. No one was telling him otherwise. He acted professionally, especially when he concluded he was wrong after all. The message of this *Chatas* offering seems to be, forgiveness is unnecessary and your dignity is already recovered.

The next recovery plan is for the *Sanhedrin*/High-Court (Lev. 4:13-21), under similar circumstances. Forgiveness is mentioned even though their error was similar to that of the *Kohen Gadol*, they thought they were correct at the time. The difference between the two cases is that, in the case of the *Kohen Gadol,* only he sinned whereas, in the case of the *Sanhedrin*, not only did they decide wrongly, **a major part of the population sinned as a result of the court's error.** (If this didn't impact a major part of the population, this special offering is not required.)

14

We must immediately recognize the high improbability of this happening! What circumstance would lead to a majority of the population acting in concert? Moreover, by what survey method would this be confirmed? Even more mystifying, how could every one of the *Sanhedrin* members be mistaken? And if it wasn't unanimous, how could it be that the minority who were correct could not muster the appropriate logic or authoritative sources to prove their position to the majority? Indeed, how did the truth finally come out? Normally, the majority opinion becomes the authoritative rule, so by definition the *Sanhedrin* cannot be mistaken. These improbabilities practically guarantee that **the circumstances leading to the *Sanhedrin* error were Divinely ordained**. It was as if Hashem was saying, "I let that happen because you needed some shakeup. Regulate yourselves more carefully. Now you are forgiven".

The next three paragraphs (Lev. 4:22-35) describe variations of a *Chatas*/Sin offering required when a member of the public committed a major sin by mistake. **Most people don't make mistakes on major issues because they rarely encounter them.** Social pressure and the daily demands of life keep them far away from major issues. Consequently, this encounter with a major issue may have been contrived by Hashem as a jarring experience to keep him much more alert against errors in the normal daily routine. The final result remains, "it will be forgiven him" - he will recover.

Next (Lev.5:1-13) appears the description of the *Chatas-Olah -V'Yored*/Sin- Offering-That-Varies-Up-and-Down, applicable in two cases:

1.   someone accidentally defiled the *Mikdash*/Sanctuary
2.   someone wilfully violated certain types of oaths.

One definite message is that **defiling the sanctity of one's personal oath is akin to defiling the public Sanctuary, revered by all**. A person has to maintain his solemn word as inviolable as Hashem's Sanctuary. It is terribly embarrassing to have been found wanting in this regard, unless the person has already lost a good deal of his self respect. Such low self respect is often the result of financial instability. I suspect that is why, particularly here, Hashem provided the **"make-it-right"** plan of *Chatas-Olah-V'Yored*/Sin-Offering-That-Varies-Up-and- Down, depending on the sinner's financial circumstances. It would be counterproductive to construct a recovery plan so expensive that it would exacerbate his financial instability, the source of his low self respect.

The poorest is allowed the least expensive *Asham*, a meal offering. Bringing the cheapest offering might itself be embarrassing. The Torah's desire to dissipate such shame might explain three textual curiosities. **First**, the Torah allowed four ways to make a meal offering and only three for either *Olah* or *Shlamim* (Lev. 1:1 - 3:17). I suggest this was done to add extra options to the poor person and extra dignity to his offering from the attention the Torah gives it.

Second, I initially did not understand why the nation's Omer offering was inserted (Lev. 2:14-16) into a parsha that otherwise deals exclusively with private offerings. I now understand that the mention of the national meal offering for the Omer conveys to the poor person's meal offering the same dignity that naturally accompanies a national offering. **Third**, the poorest sinner's inexpensive meal offering is described as "it shall belong to the Kohen like the (regular) meal offering" (Lev. 5:13). This phrase equates the poor sinner's offering with a regular meal offering which is from someone who didn't sin at all. **As a father will comfort an already crying child with** "Hush. Hush. It is over", Hashem assures the very poor man who is already suffering from financial stress but has sinned, "it will be forgiven" - you can recover.

The parsha continues with the *Asham* offerings. The normal *Asham* is for mistakenly abusing *Mikdash*/holy-things (Lev. 5:14-16). A reader familiar with all the stringent precautions that people took in Temple times to protect the Mikdash sanctity will appreciate the trauma that might accrue to one who suddenly realizes he has been deficient in this regard. Hashem mitigates such trauma with a **"make-it-right"** plan and then assures him that "it will be forgiven".

Tie-in to start: Hashem starts Vayikra by calling to Moshe who had connected so deeply with Him. The parsha continues by offering Moshe-like connections (*Olah*/Elevation, *Mincha*/Meal *and Shlomim*/Peace) for each individual to call upon Him. These **distinction opportunities** should not be taken for granted because they far surpass what we normally experience. Its modern equivalent would be for a regular citizen to have the right to express any opinion they like to his country's Senate and have it discussed there by a quorum of its members. Only Hashem could offer such access and only Hashem could expect it. When we fail to take advantage of the opportunities to call upon Hashem, He may arrange for some trip-ups (*Chatas*/Sin and *Asham*/Guilt) to occur so He can provide a recovery plan for the connection.

The Last Two Paragraphs: After the uplifting "it will be forgiven" to which we had become accustomed, **the second last paragraph tacks on an unexpectedly harsh condemnation.** The paragraph describes the *Asham-Talui*/Possibly-Guilty offering brought when the commission of the sin is in doubt. For example, he ate a piece of fat thinking it was *shuman*, the permissible type of fat. He then discovers it <u>may</u> have been *chelev*, the forbidden type of fat. Under such doubt, he brings an *Asham-Talui*/ Possibly-Guilty in case there was a sin. As the pattern has led us to expect, "it will be forgiven him", especially here where there may really have been no sin to forgive. But the next verse does an about face with the harsh*, asham hu, ashom asham la'Hashem*, "It is a guilt offering, he has become guilty guilty before Hashem" (Lev. 5:19). **Why use the GUILT word when the sin may never have taken place?** Three times!? Especially after "it will be forgiven him"?

The answer lies in the truth that Hashem not only sees all but also arranges all - all the circumstances that befall us. Isn't that how Hashem calls to us when we get absent-minded? In our example, He arranged for the uncertainty of whether the fat that the person ate was permissible or forbidden. What kind of person would Hashem subject to that dubious circumstance? The tzaddik! A tzaddik, we are taught, is normally protected from accidental sins, to help him maintain the purity he strives to achieve. But he is human, still not perfect. **How to wake him up to a subtle fault he may never realize he has while still protecting him from actually harming himself?** The answer is, cause him to think he has erred and then use the verse to shout three times, GUILTY – that will be a wake-up call he will understand.

Similarly, the very last paragraph also ends strangely, this time with the very opposite of harshness. It ends with, "it will be forgiven him for any of all the things he might do to incur guilt" (Lev. 5: 26). As I explained above, these words seem unbelievable! This person held money illegally and wilfully against the protests of the rightful owner, and when taken to court, lied under oath knowing it was a lie. **It is so surprising to learn that he is forgiven at all** since he knew every step to be wrong. Granted he has finally paid the money with a penalizing extra fifth and an *Asham,* so there has been a "make-it-right" process. Still, it should have been enough for the Torah to conclude "it will be forgiven him" as it does in most of the preceding cases where there is much less guilt. What message did the Torah intend by adding the phrase, "he is forgiven for any of all the things he might do to incur guilt"?

An answer may be found in a reconsideration of this phrase's original Hebrew, *v'nislach lo ul achas mikol asher ya'aseh l'ashma ba*. A more literal translation is "he is forgiven <u>on one</u> (rather than <u>for any</u>) of all the things that he has done to incur guilt". Sometimes a person's sin is only the tip of the iceberg; there is also greed, chutzpah and insensitivity that enabled the person to completely defy community standards. **There has to be an opening back into the community** and this *Asham's* atonement offers one. But the opening is only on the core sin, the false oath that sealed the trespass. On that, he is forgiven. But Hashem reminds him of "all the things that he has done" – the greed, the chutzpah, the insensitivity; those things still need repair. (Indeed, this last idea echoes Rambam who advises additional *Kappara* is still needed after the *Asham* due to the *Chillul Hashem* in the false oath (Hilchos Shvuos, 12:1).

This truth applies to everyone and that may be why this case was saved for last - **in the end** , there is always something to repair.

צו – Tzav

Command

8 Masoretic Paragraphs, 96 verses;
Leviticus Chapters 6 –8

Parsha 2: Command Performance

The last three verses of צו each contain the word *tzav* (in one form or another), the same word with which the parsha began, but **not many comment on this obvious tie-in**. What does attract an unusual amount of commentary is the very last verse, "Aharon and his sons carried out <u>all the matters</u> that Hashem commanded <u>through</u> Moshe" (Lev. 8:36). The commentaries pose three questions.

1. Why bother to relate that Aharon and his sons performed the commandments when we knew they would? What does it teach us?
2. The activities related here are chronologically related to the activities described at the end of parsha Pikudei (Ex. 40). There, the verses said nineteen times "just as

Hashem commanded Moshe". What more is added by the phrase kol-ha'dvorim/all-the-matters?

3. Why use the phrase b'yad Moshe, "through [the hand of] Moshe" rather than just "Moshe"?

The following review of the commentaries reveals that no one commentary resolves all three questions with a consistent theme.

Rashi seems to address the first question when he explains that this last verse functions "to praise Aharon and sons for not veering right or left" from their instructions. However, this seems weak since, in the previous verse, Moshe advised them to safeguard this charge of Hashem so that they would not die. Rashi himself interprets this as an emphatic reminder to Aharon that disobedience will result in death. Given the warning that death will result from disobedience, what great praise did Aharon deserve for avoiding death?

Gur Aryeh winds up addressing the second question during an attempt to defend the Rashi comment that I just attacked. He explains Rashi's praise of Aharon in reference to the very great many details (kol-ha'dvorim/all-the-matters) that Aharon and his sons performed without a single mistake. This required great focus and care throughout and deserves mention. The problem with Gur Aryeh's explanation is that it doesn't reflect Rashi's text which never referenced the phrase "all the matters". More pointedly, although the parsha began with detailed instructions to Aharon, the parsha ends describing the seven inauguration days of the Ohel-Moed/Tent-of- Meeting during which time, **it was**

Moshe who performed all the services. The main duty of Aharon and his sons at this time was simply to remain within the *Ohel Moed* for seven days and eat the meat and bread of the sacrifice; that was the subject of the threat of death. With that warning, what could be so hard to follow? And, again, why "*b'yad Moshe*" rather than just "Moshe"?

Gur Aryeh, himself, seems dissatisfied with the above explanation because he proceeds to offer another one. Basing himself on a *Sifra* which describes the great joy with which Aharon and his sons performed their duties, Gur Aryeh explains, "great people tend to feel resentment when they must obey instructions received through a contemporary, but Aharon had no such feelings. He performed the service dictated by Moshe with complete selflessness" (from Artscroll Stone Ed. P. 587). This answer is not in Rashi nor does Gur Aryeh suggest that it is. It does, though, **seem to answer our third question** of why the extra phrase of *b'yad Moshe*, "through Moshe" - to emphasize that Aharon's instructions came from his younger brother.

Ramban uses the last two words of the parsha, *b'yad Moshe*, to derive a surprising explanation completely opposite from Rashi. He considers the extra phrase *b'yad-Moshe*/through-Moshe as lower quality praise than just "Moshe". **Ramban contends the verse withholds complete praise** from Aharon and his sons because their behavior somehow led to the strange fire offered by two of Aharon's sons that resulted in their deaths, as related in next week's parsha (Lev. 10:1-7).

This explanation is so unusual that, despite Ramban's stature, **Ha'emek Davar completely rejects it,** citing two compelling arguments. First, Ramban does not explain why he considers *b'yad-Moshe*/through-Moshe lower quality praise than just "Moshe". It may have been obvious to him but it is not obvious to Ha'emek Davar, nor to us. Second, the strange fire was offered afterwards, on the eighth day, quite separately from the seven day inauguration rituals about which this verse is commenting.

Ha'emek Davar also focuses on the second question to offer his own explanation of the last verse. He quotes *Talmud Krisus* 13b on a verse similar to ours: "to teach the Children of Israel all the decrees that Hashem had spoken (*deebair*) to them through Moshe (*b'yad Moshe*) (Lev. 10:11). *Talmud Krisus* says that *deebair* in the verse refers to decided halacha and *b'yad Moshe* refers to *gemara*, which is derived halacha. Ha'emek Davar points out that ***deebair*** in the quoted verse has the same root as ***dvarim*** in our verse and *b'yad Moshe* is common to both verses.

Applying these concepts to understand our verse, we are being told that Aharon and his sons adhered to the decided law which Hashem had told Moshe explicitly; and also to the other laws that Moshe had not been told but had derived on his own, and this is why they are praised. Upon reflection, Ha'emek Davar is really expanding upon Rashi's approach of praising Aharon and his sons. However, he doesn't expound on how remaining in the entrance of the Tent of Meeting would have needed such a range of laws that were both explicit and derived.

We still don't have an answer for Rashi. How could Rashi suggest that Aharon and his sons were praiseworthy for avoiding a death sentence, especially when there was little they had to do? Since this parsha always happens soon before Pesach, the question becomes even more pronounced in light of the great sacrifices and stringencies that every Jew makes to accommodate Pesach. What was so unusual about Aharon's behaviour? Moreover, what can we learn from it?

It is indeed not unusual for Jews to take upon themselves all kinds of self imposed sacrifices and stringencies. **Perhaps, therein lays the answer for Rashi!** Aharon, Rashi insists, veered neither right nor left. Rashi may have been alluding to right and left in **Kabbalah** where right represents kindness and left represents judgment. Rashi meant Aharon and his sons veered neither right to kindness nor left to judgment . When we are judgmental on ourselves, we introduce *chumra's*/stringencies to be sure we stay far from breaking the law. When we are kind to ourselves, we introduce *kula's*/leniencies to make life more bearable, perhaps to synthesize more aspects of Jewish practise into a balanced life. Both attitudes have their place because they help us personalize our devotion. But in the *Ohel-Moed*/Tent-of-Meeting, so close to Hashem, the personalization must be His, not ours.

The entire tribe of Levi were renowned for their steadfast adherence to the law, i.e. Hashem's will. Rashi's point is that

Aharon and his sons were the best of them, **able to completely expunge personal decisions in deference to His decisions**. The death threat was very good reason to change the service restrictively with *chumra's*/stringencies, but Aharon and his sons did not. Moshe's license to derive law as he saw fit (*b'yad Moshe*) was tempting precedent for others to do the same, as they saw fit, but Aharon did not. Rashi highlights for us how the Torah testifies about the extraordinary capacity of Aharon and his sons to override the normal human impulse to add something to make it their own. A fitting cap to their inauguration!

We have answered all three questions by expounding Rashi's answer. Yes, we would expect Aharon and his sons to listen to Moshe just as we would ourselves. But we would never conceive of listening with such intensity as to enact every detail of *kol-ha'dvorim*/all-the-matters, without veering right or left (as Rashi remarks) especially after Moshe had laid the groundwork by introducing the changes (*b'yad Moshe*) he was authorized to do.

In closing, we learn from Aharon the full meaning of "serve". So often we accommodate each other in a way we feel ought to be enough, even when there were clear signs that something different was desired by the other person. Service of Hashem is often described to a level of detail that some might call niggling. Nevertheless, we accommodate because we recognize Hashem's power over us. Perhaps, **it was designed to train us about our own power to serve others,** to the detail they appreciate rather than the detail we think appropriate. In show business, there is a phrase "command performance". It occurs when a performer has perfected such high skill that the very elite are certain they will be well served by a performance and so they request one. Of course, once that happens, everyone wants to see a performance. We might think of Hashem's mitzvahs as guidelines for us to reach such exalted status of a command performance.

Tie-in to start: The three *tzav's* at the end of the parsha add another insight about exemplary service. At the parsha's start, Rashi explained *Tzav* as "urgency, now and forever" (Lev. 6:2). To act immediately, and always immediately, means no time was spent concocting personal strategies or styles. When we respond quickly to someone else's needs or request, they immediately feel validated. That is because **quick service is visible service.** You might say, it is the last word on service.

שמיני – Shmini

(the) Eighth

6 Masoretic Paragraphs, 91 verses;
Leviticus Chapters 9 - 11

Parsha 3: Becoming Holy

The last verse of שמיני says "to separate between the *tomai* and *tohor* and between the creature that may be eaten and the creature that may not be eaten" (Lev. 11:47). Of the two words I haven't translated in this verse, *tomai* is a negative word usually translated as impure, while *tohor* is a positive word usually translated as pure; the negative is mentioned first and then the positive. However, as we continue reading, we notice that the creatures that may or may not be eaten are described in reverse order, with the positive mentioned first before the negative? **Isn't that the wrong order?**

Mayanei shel Torah recites an answer to this question from the *Vilna Gaon* based on *Talmud Yuma* 82b which reports two incidents years apart. Both incidents revolve around the fact that a pregnant woman will sometimes experience an intense craving for a particular food which makes her ill until it is satisfied. We rule that if such a craving is for a *treif*/forbidden food, the pregnant woman is allowed to eat the *treif* food. It happened once that a pregnant woman developed a craving for a particular food on Yom Kippur. The problem wasn't that it was treif - it wasn't, the problem was that it was forbidden to eat because it was Yom Kippur. The local rabbi wasn't sure if the override allowing her to satisfy her craving with *treif* food would also allow eating on Yom Kippur - a different kind of prohibition. So, he consulted a top sage. The sage he went to was the famous author of Mishna, R. Yehudah, who also may not have been sure about the override, but had a good idea. He suggested, **"whisper in the woman's ear that it is Yom Kippur."** They did and the craving disappeared; the pregnancy proceeded normally and she bore a son who eventually became a famous sage named R. Yochanan.

Some years later, the same thing recurred. Another pregnant woman craved a certain type of food on Yom Kippur and her family asked R. Chanina if she was allowed to eat on Yom Kippur under such circumstances. Remembering the story of R. Yehudah, he suggested they whisper in her ear that it was Yom Kippur. They did but the craving persisted so they allowed her to eat. The pregnancy proceeded normally and she also bore a son but he grew into a renowned villain, Shabtai, the market manipulator.

Here is how the *Vilna Gaon* connected the above story of the pregnant women to our verse (the *Vilna Gaon* could often quote **a verse that foretold the fate of a person**). He pointed out that the Hebrew word *"chaya"*, which is correctly translated as "creature" in the verse, could hint at a secondary meaning of a "pregnant woman"; also the Hebrew word for "be eaten" could hint at a secondary meaning of "has eaten". Accordingly, the surface version of our verse "to separate between the *tomai* and *tohor* and between the creature that may be eaten and the creature that may not be eaten" also hints at the following future event, "to separate between the *tomai* [Shabtai] and *tohor* [R. Yochanan] and between the pregnant woman who has eaten [on Yom Kippur] and the pregnant woman who has not". The secondary version properly places first the *tomai* Shabtai and his mother who ate on Yom Kippur and places second the *tohor* R. Yochanan and his mother who refrained from eating.

The ingenuity of the *Vilna Gaon* ia always a marvel to behold. However, his approach may raise questions about free will if a person's future has already been foretold. Such questions can be answered by realizing that the Torah may contain more than one story option for a person; we will only recognize the story option that happens. In this way, the Torah can foretell the fate of a person **without removing free will.**

The Talmud is troubling, though, because it suggests that the future of the children in the two stories resulted from their mothers' behaviour rather than their own. That is surprising, especially since the second mother did nothing wrong; she did not seek the craving or the illness. She asked for guidance and was given permission to eat. Why would she deserve an evil son?

I suggest, **no one deserves an evil child or gets one**. The Talmud is simply describing life. The woman who can stifle or ignore a craving when reminded about Yom Kippur is one who has nursed within herself a connection to Yom Kippur, a sense of awe for the day, a source of resolve. A woman without this resolve will be unable to stifle a craving. Parents transmit their values and commitments to their children with the full hearted conviction this is what is best for their children. A mother so imbued with Yom Kippur awe that it outweighs the physical changes in her body will more likely instil the values and aspirations of a R. Yochanon into her child. A mother who needs to satisfy her physical urges will more likely instil the needs and decisions of a Shabtai into her child.

Cravings crop up, sometimes to pregnant women but at one time or another, to all of us. The *Vilna Gaon* may have told more than just a fortune; he revealed to us the Torah message that **the road to *Tahara*/purity is through self-restraint.** Good message but not the only one at the end of the parsha.

The last half of *Shmini* discusses the animals that are *tomai* to us; sometimes in the sense we cannot eat them and sometimes in the sense they convey *tuma*, ritual impurity. It may be curious that *tomai* describes both non-kosher animals and ritually impure objects, especially since both subjects are unique to the Jewish people. Both concepts of kosher and ritual impurity impact our lives profoundly, and come with numerous, numerous details. The sheer number of these details can be daunting.

Recognizing the size of the task, the Torah encouraged us in this undertaking with an **inspiring message** a few verses before the end: "For I am Hashem your Lord – you are to sanctify yourselves and be holy, for I am holy, do not contaminate yourselves through any teeming thing that creeps on the earth. For I am Hashem, Who elevated you from the land of Egypt to be for you a Lord; you shall be holy for I am holy" (Lev. 11:44-45).

What a great, motivating finish: "you shall be holy for I am holy"! Why then is it not the finish? Why did the Torah continue pedantically with verses 46-47 ("This is the instruction regarding animals, birds, etc.") which could have easily been placed earlier so as to finish with this inspiring flourish?

Furthermore, the phrase "you shall be holy, for I am holy", is repeated in two consecutive verses, 44-45 as quoted above, verses which are almost identical. Why are the repetitions of phrases and verses necessary? Rashi addresses this problem in his last comment on the parsha by justifying the repetition as referring to new information about exactly how much of the throat needs to be slit open for kosher slaughter/*shchita* and which lung lesions are not kosher/*treif*. **Quite necessary somewhere but unnecessary here** - the flourish at the end would have been more uplifting.

To answer, perhaps we should read as follows. Verse 44 starts with "I am Hashem your Lord" – that is to say: it is a fact that I am your Lord, there can be no dispute on this. Therefore, you <u>shall</u> be holy just as I am and you may not, will not, **cannot defile yourselves**. However, in reality we do defile ourselves which can make us despair of ever achieving this goal. Continues the next verse, "I am Hashem who raised you out of

Egypt to become your Lord...." That is to say: I Myself instituted a process through which I could become your Lord by rescuing you from otherwise inescapable slavery. If I went through a process, says Hashem, then you too can undergo a process and "...you can become holy just as I am holy".

What is it that we have to do? The next verse answers: "this is the Torah of .... " which Rashi explains means learn the myriad details of Torah instruction. Rather than leave us with a flourish that would inspire us when we read it, the **Torah leaves us with a working strategy**. Not the fuzzy feeling from a cursory reading, but the studying, the knowing, the understanding, of the many, many details in the Torah make us *kodosh*, holy.

This works to make us holy because holy simply means separate. When Hashem calls Himself holy it means He is in a completely separate category from everything else. It is so difficult for us to comprehend Hashem's level of separation the verse repeats it three times, holy, holy, holy (Is. 6:3), setting up a never ending pattern (the minimum number to set up a pattern is three). We can rightly conclude that what makes Hashem unendingly holy is that He knows EVERYTHING. **Knowledge always separates.** Amongst ourselves, we certainly separate based on knowledge. We say "it is not what you know, but who you know" but it is really both. Any kind of knowledge separates; Torah true knowledge separates and elevates.

That is why Rashi refers us to the details of what is kosher and what not. We could easily follow stringencies to ensure we are eating kosher. That would suffice for staying kosher. But it

would not give us knowledge of what really is kosher and what is not, so it would <u>not</u> make us holy. Becoming expert in the subtle variations – that is the way to become *Kedoshim*, holy.

The parsha is named after its third word *Shmini* which means eighth. "Eighth" immediately brings to mind the eighth day of circumcision through which every Jewish boy is **inaugurated into Hashem's covenant with us**. In our parsha, the word *Shmini*/eighth identifies Aharon's first performance as Kohen Gadol in the Holy Mishkan. This inaugurated an intimate relationship between Hashem and the Jewish people that would be permanent because it did not depend on the unusual holiness of a Moshe or Aharon but rather on the exalted office of *Kohen Gadol*. Lesser men than Moshe and Aharon could and would occupy the office and still maintain the aura it projects similar to the way we speak today of the office of the President or Prime Minister, even when we oppose the occupant.

As Moshe expected, inaugurating the office required the loss of human life to showcase the awesome dimension of Hashem's Holiness (Lev. 10:3) so that lesser men wouldn't take it for granted. Death introduces us to *tomai*/impurity as a fact of life. The struggle to overturn *tomai* into *tohor* often teaches us to exercise caution and self-restraint, as the *Vilna Gaon* explained through the stories of the two pregnant women. But caution and self-restraint is not the objective of life - Mishkan Holiness is - and every Jew can gain such Holiness by engaging with the awesome details of Hashem's Torah.

Shmini ends with a more permanent method of becoming holy like Hashem.

תזריע – Tazria
She Conceives

9 Masoretic Paragraphs, 67 verses;
Leviticus Chapters 12 - 13

Parsha 4: Understanding Tzaraas Today

Before examining the end of תזריע, we have to define the
Hebrew word *tzaraas* which is the subject of most of this
parsha and the next. ***Tzaraas* is a spiritual disease** that
manifests in physical symptoms and, as such, is not an easy
word to translate. That is why Artscroll does not bother and
simply transliterates the Hebrew letters, as do I. The original
English translation, the King James Version, translated it as
"leprosy" or "plague" which gave it the identity of a physical
disease. This led to a scoffing of the Torah when science
advanced far enough to show that the remedies described in
the Torah were useless against leprosy or plague. Thankfully,
the New International Version has recognized this error and
now has not only dropped the words "leprosy" and "plague"
but also includes the word "defiling" in the translation which
implies something spiritual rather than physical.

Tzaraas is a spiritual disease caused by sin not by a physical
abnormality in the body. This spiritual disease can appear in

three areas, 1) on a person's body, 2) a garment (wool, linen or leather), or 3) a house. *Talmud Arachin* 16a explains that any of these forms of **tzaraas can result from one of seven sins: 1)** *loshon hora* (bad mouthing someone), 2) spilling blood, 3) taking an oath in vain, 4) illicit relations, 5) haughtiness, 6) theft and 7) stinginess (a slightly different list appears in *Midrash Raba*). **The real remedy requires repenting** from these sins. The remedial actions described in the Torah are designed to assist the sinner in striving for such repentance.

Now, to the end of תזריע. The last paragraph describes what happens when *tzaraas* appears in the second area, a garment. *Oznaim LaTorah* points out that this is an interruption of the discussion about *tzaraas* in the first area, a person's body. Since introducing the subject of *tzaraas* near the beginning of our parsha, the Torah has been explaining what to do when it appears on a human and this subject continues, in the next parsha, with the instructions of how to purify oneself after the *tzaraas* has disappeared from the body. Right in the middle of these two sections appears this last paragraph of our parsha which describes everything that must be done with *tzaraas* on a garment. **Why didn't the Torah first finish discussing** *tzaraas* **of a person's body before digressing to** *tzaraas* **of a garment?**

Oznaim LaTorah provides a Kabbalistic answer which mostly focuses on why *tzaraas* only appears to garments of wool, linen and leather and ties this into the *loshon hora* spoken against Hashem by the serpent in the story of the original sin in Gan Eden (see P. 188 of Vol. 3 of "Insights in the Torah", Artscroll

Mesorah Series). However, I could not discern from his answer anything we can learn about our own lives. **I present a less mystical answer** that may be more helpful.

Nobody is perfect and we all try to hide our faults. *Tzaraas*, on the other hand, is a very public condition – the kohen must see it and declare it *tzaraas.* Until then, it is nothing. Not only that, the person has to remove himself from society and warn anybody who comes near that he is *tamei.* With this in mind, it would be very tempting for someone with *tzaraas* to try to hide his condition by covering it with his clothes and not show it to a kohen. But this will remove the incentive to correct the sin which caused the *tzaraas.* Therefore, the Torah interrupted the description of human *tzaraas* with garment *tzaraas* to warn that **if a person tries to hide his *tzaraas* with his clothes, he will not succeed** because it will then appear on the very clothes he is using to hide his affliction.

That explains the interrupted presentation of *tzaraas*: bodily, garment, bodily. **However, we should not yet be satisfied with our analysis. Look again at the list of 7 sins that cause *tzaraas*:**

1. *loshon hora*,
2. spilling blood,
3. taking an oath in vain,
4. illicit relations,
5. haughtiness,
6. theft and
7. stinginess.

Spilling blood (*shfichus damim*) and illicit relations (*gilu'i arayos*) are two of the three worst crimes; **why** isn't the third one of idol worship (*avodah zara*) included? **Why** are haughtiness and stinginess included when they are not even sins, just undesirable attitudes? **Why** not include other serious sins like violating *Sabbath*, eating *chametz* on *Pesach*, ignoring *Taharas Mishpacha*, and so on? Finally, **why** does the list begin with *loshon hora* and not the top sin, spilling blood?

Change the last question to a statement and we have an answer for all the questions: *Loshon Hora* begins the list because it is the most serious sin. In fact, it seems according to Rambam, **loshon hora is the only cause for *Tzaraas*** (*Hilchos Tumas Tzaraas* 16:10) because he treats the other items on the list as examples of how *loshon hora* can inadvertently lead to a revenge killing, to illicit pursuits or the like. For Rambam, the list of sins dramatizes the consequences of *loshon hora*, not that one personally committed the actual crime of murder or the like. Indeed, the Talmud had earlier been discussing the various evils of *loshon hora*; the list of seven should be seen as more of the same. Alternatively, it may be assigning the severity of these sins to *loshon hora,* meaning it is like murder because it so embarrasses a person that it drains the blood from his face, and it is like illicit relations because it uncovers the privacy of a person, and so on. In any case, only *loshon hora* causes *tzaraas*.

The Torah's third type of *tzaraas* appears on a house, following the same logic described above. Given the embarrassing circumstances surrounding a declaration of *tzaraas,* a person could attempt to avoid all this by hiding in his house, even after his garments are affected, and never confront his underlying sin. Against this strategy, the Torah warns that his house will be infected, will have to be demolished, and there will be no place left to hide. **One might as well face up to his faults early,** endure the embarrassment and make the necessary changes or things will keep getting worse. In addition to the embarrassment of bodily *tzaraas,* a person could suffer the loss of his clothes and house in the process.

To me, the above logic explaining the sequence and interruption of bodily, garment and house *tzaraas* seems reasonable. Nevertheless, I may have to reject it in deference to **Rambam who claims the reverse happens.** Rambam says (ibid), *tzaraas* first appears on the house and, if no correction is forthcoming, then on the clothes and then on the person. This Rambam is quite surprising. Not only does it contradict the reasonable order I presented above but it also is the exact opposite of the sequence presented in the Torah! Furthermore, it contradicts the most famous case of *tzaraas,* that of Miriam who was immediately afflicted on her body with no hint of a prior house or garment affliction. The only support I could find for Rambam's sequence was *Midrash VaYikra Raba* 17:4 which describes the same order of *tzaraas* on house, then garment and then body. This doesn't resolve the contradictions to this sequence from the Torah, it just bumps it up the hierarchy ladder to an earlier source.

The answer may come from another surprising part of Rambam. The verse "he will be brought to Aaron the Kohen" (Lev. 13:2) implies a duty to come to the Kohen (as per *Minchas Chinuch # 169*). However, **Rambam does not consider it a duty to present a *tzaraas* spot to the Kohen** for inspection. In Rambam's construction (*Hilchos Tumas Tzaraas 1*), the mitzvah only instructs what to do if and when someone presents a spot to the Kohen for inspection. Since Rambam maintains that one is not duty bound to present to the Kohen, **then hiding it was no sin** and should not necessarily result in escalating appearances of *tzaraas* from person to clothes to house. Thus, Rambam's reverse order is consistent with his definition of the mitzvah. Still, it doesn't explain why Rambam chose that order or why he omitted the duty to present for inspection.

Perhaps Rambam does not mean to override the plain reading of the Torah text, but to add to it. After all, there are all kinds of sinners and different treatments are required. In every treatment, **Hashem does not seek to punish sinners but to reform them, or better, to get them to reform themselves.**

Some only sin rarely such as a *tzaddik*/righteous person. When they sin, they want to immediately recover. They may even want to become an example to others by accepting public humiliation because their public image is not their goal, serving Hashem is. Such was the case of Miriam, whose affliction Rambam describes separately from his description of how *tzaraas* normally appears in stages (which supports this interpretation). **Others,** not quite so exceptional, will also respond quickly to censure but **would be devastated by public embarrassment**. The Torah allows them to reform privately and recover from afflictions through *Tshuva*. However - warns the Torah by interrupting bodily *tzaraas* with garment *tzaraas* - relapses could result in a combination of bodily and garment *tzaraas* leading to public exposure. Such warning may be enough for this kind of sinner. These are the ones described by the Torah narrative.

Some sin regularly. Still, they are human and Hashem desires their free-will choices to better themselves. If they were to experience the relentless exposure through body, then garment, then house *tzaraas* described above, they would be overwhelmed by the experience. Either they would act under compulsion, not through free choice, or they might act mindlessly, missing the point entirely. **These are the ones described by Rambam.** Better for them to first be goaded into protecting their money and show-pieces before their very person is assailed.

With this explanation of the parsha end, *tzaraas* **loses its other-world quality and becomes a template for us "moderns".** We are even further removed from Hashem than the sinners described by Rambam so our free will cannot co-exist with any sequence of *tzaraas*. Consequently, *tzaraas* is absent today. But Hashem still wants to guide us. We would do well to remember this analysis when experiencing the various embarrassments, private horrors, financial setbacks and personal losses by which Hashem, to this day, continues to guide us away from self-demolition and towards exceptional achievement. **In the end,** that will be worth it.

מצורע – Metzora
The One Afflicted

7 Masoretic Paragraphs, 90 verses;
Leviticus Chapters 14 - 15

Parsha 5: Why *Loshon Hora* is the Worst Sin

The last phrase of מצורע describes a man who is intimate with a woman while she is *tmai'ah*/impure, a sinful act. The placing of this phrase contradicts a statement of the Vilna Gaon in his commentary on the four sons of the Pesach Haggada. According to the Vilna Gaon, the Haggada wishes to contrast two sets of people. (In the following, I have used different translations than the usual ones to convey a sense of the message the Vilna Gaon derives from his order.) The *chacham*/wise son is contrasted with the *sh'eino-yodai'a-li'shol*/son-who-doesn't-realize-the-value-of-asking while the *tam*/pure-minded son is contrasted with the *rasha*/evil-minded son. However, according to this analysis, the *rasha*/evil-minded son should have been placed at the end of the list instead of in the middle. He acknowledges this and explains the author of the Haggada **did not wish to end the list on a bad note**, namely the *rasha*. But, couldn't the author of the Haggada follow the example of our

46

parsha which ends on the sinful act of intimacy with a *tmai'ah?*

A simple and obvious solution is to assume the Vilna Gaon would accept the following amendment: Do not end on a derogatory note... unless there is a reason to do so. Such an amendment would deflect any question from our last word since Rabbeinu Bachya suggests our parsha ends with *tmai'ah* for a good reason, it clarifies a mystery. The very next verse (which begins next week's parsha) recalls the fact that Aharon's sons died but no verse ever declared explicitly why they died. Rabbeinu Bachya suggests that our last word **tmai'ah alludes to the reason they died** in the next story, because they entered the Mishkan while *tamai*. However, to reconcile with the commentaries who give other reasons for their death, ending with the bad word *tmai'ah* remains a problem for the Vilna Gaon.

A better solution is to realize that the last phrase may describe a sinful act but it is the intimacy which was the sin and intimacy is not the last word. *Tmai'ah* is the last word and it is not the negative term that *rasha* is. **There is no sin in becoming *tamei*** just as there is no sin in becoming dirty, just a preference to remain clean. Sometimes, there is a need, almost a duty, to become *tamei* such as the case of a woman who has given birth, as described at the beginning of *Tazria* (Lev. 12:1-8). Surely, bearing children is a sacred accomplishment. So is burying the dead but both result in being *tamei*. *Tamei* may be a negative offset to *tohor* but it is not a sin.

The realization that *tamei* is not sinful helped me solve another difficulty at the end of our parsha which I found much more troubling.

Metzora ends with the same subject that started the previous parsha, *Tazria*, namely, the subject of *tuma*/impurity arising from the reproductive organs. The subject of *tzaraas* is an interruption, as follows:

Parsha	Chapter:Verse	*Tuma* Subject
Tazria	12:1-8	Reproductive organs (giving birth)
	13:1-46	*Tzaraas* (of body)
	13:47-59	*Tzaraas* (of garment)
Metzora	14:1-32	*Tzaraas* (of body purified)
	14:33-57	*Tzaraas* (of house)
	15:1-33	Reproductive organs (discharging)

Just as *Oznaim LaTorah* asked at the end of *Tazria* why the Torah interrupted the subject of bodily *tzaraas* with the details of garment *tzaraas,* we should ask here, why did the Torah interject the whole subject of *tzaraas* <u>right in the middle</u> of telling us about *tuma*/impurity arising from the reproductive organs? **This is so unusual, it must lead to a message!**

R. Shimshon R. Hirsch provides a message; one even deeper than it at first appears. He describes the subjects of **Family Purity and *loshon hora* in terms of the unbridled passion** that accompanies each. Our reproductive organs often dominate the physical, animal side of our existence. They drive a large chunk of our behavior which we often come to regret. Even when we suspect we will regret the behavior we are about to engage, we all too often feel powerless to resist. The laws of Family Purity suggest by their very existence that we need not be enslaved by these drives. These same laws guide us to strategies by which we can control these drives. Some question Hashem, "Why implant such passion within us and then expect us to overcome it?" The answer is: **To be in control is to be like Hashem.**

Our social chatter is also a passion of similar pervasiveness. We gossip among ourselves because we feel we need to know who is the leader and who not? Who is successful and who not? Who is acceptable and who not? And so on. By enfolding the details of *tzaraas* within those of Family Purity, the Torah acknowledges that, despite the threat of resulting *tzaraas,* our inclination to commit *loshon hora* is as natural and powerful as our sex drive. The Torah also sends a message. **Here too we can master the passion.** We can emulate Hashem, be in control and not speak *loshon hora.*

The ability to achieve such self-control would be truly sublime. It will no doubt **require many encounters with the hidden workings of our mind.** That may explain why the Torah chose to teach us this lesson through mysterious *tzaraas* with all its strange details. One example of these strange details is the Torah's introduction of four shades of white which can appear on the body. The Sages explain there are really two basic shades, each with a derivative, and any of the four can combine together to qualify for the minimum size required. This leaves unanswered the question, why introduce four shades, or two shades, just say white?! The message is that we have to encounter the mysteries in order to gain control.

Loshon hora lends itself to this exercise because it is also mysterious, on several fronts. For one, what is *loshon hora?* The colloquial use of the term *loshon hora* encompasses three halachik concepts, *motzi shem ra, loshon hora,* and *rechilus.* The first two describe an act of communicating a negative quality about someone. When the communication is a lie, it is called *Motzi shem ra,* and when it is true it is called *loshon hora.* Many people are now familiar with these two terms.

Less well known is *Rechilus*, no doubt because of the different definitions offered by the early authorities.

Early Authority	Definition of *Rechilus*	Problem with Definition
Rabbeinu Yona *Shaarei Tshuva* III, 55	Issues a derogatory report about a fellow Jew	Uses the same words that define *motzi shem ra*
Rambam *Hilchos Deos* 7:2	Reports what he heard people say or what he heard said about people, even if true	Doesn't mention that it is derogatory or concerning the people listening, so it seems Rambam forbids newspapers
Raavad ibid (as described by *Kesef Mishna*)	Same as above except the report includes the action that the person reported said he was going to take against the listener	Really just a subset of *loshon hora* because it is a bad report about someone
SMa"G Neg. 11	Reveals to listener what someone said about him in secret	What if it was good? What if it wasn't good but it wasn't said in secret; the listener just hadn't heard about it
Chinuch Mitzvah 236	Reporting something bad a person said about the listener	Does not distinguish between *motzi shem ra, loshon hora,* and *rechilus*
Chofetz Chaim Hilchos Isurei Rechilus Klal 1, 2-3	Reporting to listener what a person said of or did to the listener even if the person does not mind being reported upon	What if it was good?

All of the above are different upon analysis. Today, most everybody acknowledges the authority in this matter of the Chofetz Chaim but I find the text of his definition unclear. The sum of his rulings is perhaps best expressed by Note 16 on P.661 of Artscroll Stone Chumash:

***Rechilus* is telling someone what others have said or done behind his back, if there is even the slightest possibility that it may cause ill will.**

I encourage everyone to memorize this statement for guidance in action and education, due to the wide range of formulas cited. I also point out a safety valve. **If the names of the people spoken about are not mentioned and are not discoverable from context, none of the three prohibitions apply.**

We are not done. Even after clearly defining *loshon hora* it remains a mystery why it is condemned the way it is. Says Talmud Yerushalmi: "There are four sins for which punishment is exacted in this world but the primary punishment is left for the World to Come: idol worship, illicit relations and spilling of blood – and *loshon hora* is equal to them all" (Peah 4a). Not only, says the Yerushalmi, is it like one personally committed a <u>capital</u> crime; it is as if one committed all three of the worst capital crimes! This beggars the imagination. **How can a common human foible, practised far and wide, be considered the worst crime against society?**

The language of the Yerushalmi might give us a clue because it echoes the language of the famous *mishna*: "These are the precepts whose fruits a person enjoys in this world but whose principle remains intact for enjoyment in the World to Come......and the study of Torah is equal to all of them" (Peah 1:1). The similarity of language implies that just as we expect

Torah study to guide us toward good so too we should expect *loshon hora* to guide us toward bad. **How might it do that?**

The answer lies in realizing that life, itself, is always a mystery unfolding. "What will make me worthwhile?" is a question that dogs us at every turn. The Torah tugs us one way, "Follow this path and you will reach an end reward that will totally delight you especially since, currently, it is imperceptible". *Loshon hora* tugs us another, "Forget the end reward which can't be seen. Look around right now and be satisfied with how much better you are than the other fellow who has such and such faults that you don't". **The ability to validate oneself on a social scale blocks the inspiration one can derive from a Torah scale.**

Instead of striving to emulate Hashem, one behaves as if there were no such goal – surely a decision one will come to rue in the World to Come. When we measure ourselves by social norms instead of Divine goals, our world remains what society is, and the **World to Come can never come**. Inevitably, this destroys the end goal of Creation – the real purpose of society.

The last comment can help us end on a positive note, as the Vilna Gaon would wish, because it leads to an answer for one nagging question that persists. If *loshon hora* is as terrible a crime as painted, why aren't there more expositions on it in the Talmud and *Rishonim*? It was not until recently that the Chofetz Chaim wrote the definitive works on the subject – making it seem like a recent stringency, *chalilah*.

Such doubts can be quieted if my insight above rings true - *loshon hora* **stops the World to Come from coming.** Perhaps the reason we didn't have such emphasis on the subject earlier in Jewish history was because the World to Come was not yet near. In contrast, many sages have lately encouraged us that we may be on the cusp of messianic times. For the very reason that the time is ripe, now is when we need a better grasp on what is holding us back. Accordingly, it was the Chofetz Chaim of recent times who was inspired to finally write the rule book on the subject rather than an earlier authority.

In reference back to the last words of the parsha, we have been intimate with *tuma* long enough. If we self-control, we can live in messianic times. **So be careful. No names.**

אחרי מות – Acharei Mos

After the Death

7 Masoretic Paragraphs, 80 verses;
Leviticus Chapters 16 - 18
Parsha 6: Recovering From Stumbling

The last seven verses of אחרי מות should infuriate me with the contradiction they introduce but, instead, I am humbled by the extra level of sophistication they reveal. In my discussion of the previous parsha, Metzora, I had made the bold claim that there is no sin in being *tamei*. These last seven verses contradict me with *tamei* that results from sins of immorality. Loathe to retract a lesson I have taught, I launched into an investigation that revealed the **Torah bounces back and forth between sinful and sin-less *tamei***, as follows:

Source	Trigger	Result
Parsha Shmini, Lev. 11:4 "it is *tamei* to you"	eating non-kosher, e.g. camel	sinful *tamei*
Parsha Shmini, Lev. 11:24 "through this you become *tamei*"	contact with animal carcass	sin-less *tamei*
Parsha Shmini, Lev. 11:44 "...you shall be *kodosh* (holy) because I am *kodosh*, do not make your souls *tamei* with all that swarms on the earth"	eating non-kosher	sinful *tamei*
Parsha Tazria, Lev. 12:1 "gives birth to a male, she shall be *tamei*..."	childbirth	sin-less *tamei*
Parsha Tazria, Lev. 13:3 "the kohen shall look and declare him *tamei*"	*tzaraas* of various types	sin-less *tamei* (although *tzaraas* results from sins such as *loshon hora*, its *tamei* comes from skin lesions, not sin)
Parsha Metzora, Lev. 14:2 "on the day of his becoming *tohor*..."	*tzaraas* purification	*tohor* from sin-less *tamei*
Parsha Metzora, Lev. 15:2 "...his discharge is *tamei*"	discharges from reproductive organs	sin-less *tamei*
Parsha Acharei Mos, Lev. 18:20 "...to make yourself *tamei* with her"	immorality, unions not subject to *kiddushin*	sinful *tamei*
Parsha Kedoshim, Lev. 19:2 "you shall be *kodosh*"	do mitzvahs	not sins leading to *tamei*

Sin-less types of *tamei* require a process to become *tohor* before entering places of *kodosh*, especially the Sanctuary, and before eating *kodosh* foods such as *terumah* and sacrificial meat. To exit such a state of *tamei* one must perform the appropriate *tohor* process. In contrast, **sinful** *tamei* does not have a *tohor* process with a definite end; its remedy is *teshuva* and *kappara* which can last a lifetime. It also does not bar entry to places of *kodosh*. Instead, it denies any sort of *kedusha* to forbidden unions and diminishes a sinner's personal sense of *kodosh*. The following table summarizes this.

	Sin-less *tamei*	Sinful *tamei*
Kodosh	cannot enter	opposite of
Remedy	tohor process	teshuva, kappara
Dichotomy	*tamei/tohor*	*tamei/kodosh*

The Torah has identified two dichotomies, namely, *Tamei/Tohor* and *Tamei/Kodosh*. These two dichotomies need not be viewed as novel because they are a continuation of the Yom Kippur theme introduced earlier in *Acharei Mos*. Yom Kippur is the day for human regeneration! Its bull offerings atone for having entered the Sanctuary while unknowingly impure (Rashi Lev. 16:11), a *Tamei/Tohor* situation; its goat offerings together with both *teshuva* and the power of the day atone for sins (Rambam Hilchos Teshuva, Ch. 1:2), a *Tamei/Kodosh* situation. That is why only when explaining

Yom Kippur are the two positive concepts of *tohor* and *kodosh* mentioned together (Lev. 16:19).

But, having earlier standing does not take away the obvious question. **How can the one concept of *tamei* have two different opposites?** A less obvious but equally intriguing question follows.

With the identification of *Tamei/Tohor* and *Tamei/Kodosh*, we have a third instance of an interruption in content continuity. Remembering that the first two instances uncovered hidden messages, we are entitled to ask what might be the hidden message here.

In the first instance, the last paragraph of *Tazria* **interrupted** the subject of bodily *Tzaraas* with that of a garment. This led to an understanding of the different sequences of severity by which Hashem may chastise us. For example, a tzaddik might get an overly severe punishment right away because he wants to correct himself and his world as soon as possible, but a regular person, who may become too depressed with such a display of rejection, is better served with a private setback.

In the second instance, at the end of *Metzorah* we noticed the entire subject of *Tzaraas* **interrupted** the subject of *Taharas Mishpacha* with which Parsha *Tazria* started and Parsha *Metzorah* ended. This realization led to an appreciation of our need and capacity to exercise equal control over two of our most powerful urges, physical intimacy and social bonding.

Now, **in a third instance**, we see that the entire subject of *Tamei/Tohor* is, itself, an **interruption** of *Tamei/Kodosh*, a subject that began in Parsha *Shmini* and finished in Parsha *Acharei Mos*. Maybe one is enveloped within the other to make sure we discover a new insight. What is the message?

One message may derive from the **invisibility of these three states** of *Tamai, Tohor* and *Kodosh*. Why did Hashem create these three states that we cannot sense, not with our sight, our smell or our touch? Since whatever Hashem created was for our benefit, knowing there are invisible things must be helpful. From the outset, it certainly humbles us to know we cannot see everything. Recognizing our own ignorance is a well-known step towards maturity and that is always welcome.

Some things of which we are ignorant in the physical world we call silent killers. Cancer is a good example in that we are often unaware of its growth until it is too late. Carbon monoxide is another example of a silent killer which is physical. Sometimes, the danger is not physical. **A wrong attitude can also kill us.** Clinically acute and/or chronic depression can drive us to suicide; similarly, extreme arrogance can lead us into fatal situations.

The same can be said for less intense versions of the wrong attitude. Temporary depression can rob us of the will to achieve while a bout of arrogance can rob us of the opportunity to change course. No one can see these attitudes but they can easily destroy the moment, the entire day, or worse. The two sets of opposites, *Tamei/Tohor* and

Tamei/Kodosh, the Torah's example of things we cannot see, might give us an insight to where these attitudes come from and what we can do about them.

While pursuing our own human development, **we often stumble**, in two ways. Sometimes we stumble over life's experiences of sickness, death and other misfortunes. Some of these misfortunes develop from initiatives we took that turn out to have been false starts that led nowhere. Looking back, we sometimes wonder what possessed us to even think it might work out. When that happens we should recognize it as clear evidence of all the things learned along the way that now gives us the hindsight we lacked before. Other times, it was a reasonable gamble that unfortunately didn't work. Either way, we feel frustrated over time and effort wasted. We can easily become depressed.

These are similar to *Tamei/Tohor* situations wherein we did nothing wrong. Usually becoming *tamei* was an unavoidable event just as is sickness or the loss of a loved one. Occasionally, we may have become *tamei* by choice such as when we attend to a dead stranger because it was a mitzvah. Although it was the right thing to do, we still feel depressed, sullied and diminished. In such a state, we do not belong in *Kodosh*, a Temple that celebrates the perfect Creator. We cannot see perfection in Creation in such a state of *tamei* just as we cannot celebrate life when we are sick or grieving. To remove this *tamei* we need to take steps to become *tohor*. For a *Metzorah* these steps are to see a Kohen, immerse in a mikveh and wait for a new day. We gain insight from these rules on how to escape despondency or depression. We may need to learn how to avoid a certain situation (as taught by, see a Kohen), we certainly need to regain a positive outlook (as taught by, cleanse in a mikveh) and let time heal the wound (as taught by, wait for a new day).

The second way we stumble is through our own choices which turn out to have been harmful. Usually there were warning signs that we ignored due to our own passion or arrogance. When we finally come to our senses, we again feel frustrated over time and effort wasted, but worse, we are also somewhat broken. Our theory of what is best has been shattered. We need to change course as soon as possible but the fix is not clear.

These are similar to *Tamei/Kodosh* situations wherein we sinned. The Torah requires us to atone for sin in a three stage process:

1   stop sinning
2   regret the sin
3   commit never to repeat the sin

The Torah also requires a three part confession that gives expression to the above:

1   articulate the error, e.g. "I sinned by doing such and such"
2   express regret for having sinned, the more expressions, the better
3   express the commitment to never repeat the sin

Both of the above have three parts. Take a moment to realize the message of a three-peat. A three-peat is needed because three is the minimum number we need to recognize a pattern that will keep going. For example, if we see a series of numbers - say 1,2 – we don't know whether the next number is 3 or 4. It might be 3 because we added 1 to 1 to get 2 so next we add 1 to 2 to get 3. Or it might be 4 because we doubled 1 to get 2 so we should double 2 to get 4. But if we see a series of three number – say 1,2,3 – we know the next number must be 4, and so on to 5, 6, 7, etc. because each number is one greater than the previous. If the series of numbers we see is 1,2,4 then we know the next number is 8, followed by 16,32, etc. because each number is double the previous one. Whatever the pattern, it continues forever. Thus, the message of a three-peat is that **walking back from sin requires a never ending pattern**.

Interestingly, the last three words of our parsha become a thrice repeated mantra in the next parsha by being the last three words in each of three of its opening verses. These three words translate into "I am / the Eternal / your Lord" and they gain their significance from the admonition "you shall be holy because I am holy" (Lev. 19:2). From this we may discover that the Torah's three-peat walk-back from sin not only has a one-two punch of atonement and confession, but also a third element, namely, to **find an alternative activity.** The Torah's remedy for sin is to first drop the *tamei*, harmful choices can't be fixed; they have to be vacated. Next, speak it out so that you hear your own commitment. Then, pursue a *kodosh* activity — <u>any *kodosh* activity</u> can and will serve as an antidote. It will end the *tamei*.

קדושים – Kedoshim

Holy Ones

4 Masoretic Paragraphs, 64 verses;
Leviticus Chapters 19 - 20

Parsha 7: Is That Old Time Magic Still Here?

The last verse of קדושים leads to a debate about that old time magic. Was it **Harry Houdini type illusions** created by smoke and mirrors or was it **real power of the Harry Potter type** e.g. broomstick flying and ghosts? The verse says, "When any man or woman shall engage themselves with *Ov* or *Yidoni*, they shall surely be put to death, by stone shall they pelt them, their blood is upon them" (Lev. 20:27).

The Torah used our parsha to first raise the topic of magic. It heightened our awareness of this topic by sprinkling **three separate verses about *Ov* and *Yidoni*** around the parsha (Lev. 19:31; 20:6 and 27) rather than collapsing them together into one place, as would have been expected. Another way that the Torah highlighted the topic was by making the last verse of our parsha the source for two famous Talmudic expositions (1. differentiating between capital punishment and *Korais* for the same violation and, 2. assigning the method of stoning to any capital crime for which the verse mentions "the violator's blood").

However, the parsha of Shoftim might be a more complete source for the Torah's view on magic because it **enumerates eight prohibitions** (Deut. 18:10-11). They are, *Kosem* (fortune telling via crystal ball, etc.), *Onen* (astrology), *Mnachesh* (deciding by omen), *Kishuf* (magic that defies nature), *Chover* (incantations over animals or insects), asking *Ov*, asking *Yidoni* (i.e. asking for information from the person practising *Ov* or *Yidoni*), and *Doresh el HaMaisim* (asking the dead for advice or information).

What is *Ov* and *Yidoni*? With minor variations, the early authorities describe these practices as methods of conjuring a supernatural voice from either the ground or from within oneself for the purpose of answering questions. Were these voices and other magical acts real (Harry Potter) or illusory (Harry Houdini)?

As his comments in the parsha (Lev. 19:31) and related Talmudic sections imply, **Rashi viewed these voices as real**, but evil and therefore forbidden. Ramban and Chinuch seem to agree and ascribe the magical powers to *Koach-HaTumah/*impure-forces that are evil and dangerous. Rashi, Ramban and Chinuch would contend that we have better sources of power through the Torah.

Rambam, on the other hand, explains they are forbidden because they are examples of idol worship, i.e. completely false. Just as idols are a completely false premise, so too are these various practitioners of magic. Whatever they make appear to happen is really just an illusion (Hilchos Avoda Zara, Ch. 6). After discussing the details of these prohibitions, Rambam lectures us on the total falsehood and emptiness of these activities (Hilchos Avoda Zara, Ch. 11). His opinion finds support from the context of our parsha, Kedoshim, where the subject is *Kedusha* - be holy because I am holy, says Hashem over and over. Since Hashem is the only reality, anything opposite Hashem is not real. Thus, when our parsha labels *Ov* and *Yidoni* as *Tomai* (Lev. 19:31), it categorizes them as the opposite of Hashem, which must mean they are nothing. The verse implies the reason not to turn to them is not because we have better, **the reason is they are useless** – exactly what Rambam said.

Surprisingly, **the context in Shoftim is different enough to argue there is a real *Koach-HaTumah*/impure-force** which supports the position of Rashi, Ramban and Chinuch. To wit, after listing the prohibited activities in Shoftim, the Torah cautions not to bother with them because Hashem has provided better information and guidance through a prophet. The implication is that while these activities will work, they are not for us. We have better tools.

An amazing conclusion can be drawn from the above analysis of, Kedoshim and Shoftim, the two parshas that forbid magic. **The Torah has fostered this dispute about magic**, real or illusory, by splitting the discussion into two parshas with different contexts. Why does the Torah support such ambivalence on the subject? The answer must be that both viewpoints are useful.

Rambam's viewpoint is useful, as follows. **The spell of magic haunts us still**, its allure is not confined to the past. The modern mind may reject the idea of witches, ghosts and magic spells but, nevertheless, the fortune telling industry is big business (see the ads in the back of many magazines). Those people who smile bemusedly at these ads might check themselves first by asking how often they have tried the latest fad. Despite the absence of supporting evidence, people flock to the new diet, exercise, investment or the like, that promises to (magically?!) solve all problems. No one suggests these fads are forbidden by the Torah just as no one denies there is a persistent temptation to find easy solutions to nagging problems. Acknowledging that such temptations seem irresistible, the Torah mentioned *Ov, Yidoni* and others to teach us **Rambam's message - there are no magic formulas.**

The value of Rashi, Ramban and Chinuch can be discovered by considering **the flip side of magic, namely, the reality of Hashem**. R. Shlomo Wolbe in *Alei Shur* Vol. I, P. 311 quotes a famous *Mechilta* about the crossing of the *Yam-Suf*/Sea-of-Reeds , "a maidservant at the *Yam Suf* had a greater vision than Yechezkel the prophet". R. Wolbe asks, "how could that have been possible?" Yechezkel's vision was one of the most sublime ever. He saw the Throne of Glory! Moreover, his lifelong experience with Torah and mitzvahs must have given him a tremendously sophisticated appreciation of whatever he saw. **How could a recently freed slave of little education and shallow background have embraced a greater prophetic**

vision?

R. Wolbe's answer, which I present in a slightly different nuance, is derived from Talmud Sabbath . "This is my Gd and I will beautify Him" (Ex.15, 2). The Hebrew word *Anvehu/*beautify-Him can be split apart to form the phrase *Ani-Ve-Hu/*I-and-Him, meaning I can make myself like Gd, I can emulate Him (Sabbath 133a). The Talmud is explaining that the revelation that came at *Yam Suf* changed the maid servant's life. It showed her and taught her she could be God-like. In contrast to her, Yechezkel was already God-like due to his sophistication in the ways of Hashem. His vision of the Throne of Glory made him even more sophisticated – but that was just more of the same. In contrast, **the maid servant's vision was a life changer**, it inspired her to become much more than she was before. Although less sophisticated, her vision led to a more profound effect on her.

The different effects on Yechezkel and the maidservant from their vision remind us Hashem is too different, too infinite, too *Kodosh* to be perceived in any one way. As each of us strives to understand Hashem there will be many gaps in our understanding just because there is an infinite amount to know. Each such gap can become a question, a question can become a doubt, and **a doubt, any doubt, becomes a demon gnawing at us**, tearing away at our convictions. That is the *Koach HaTumah*. In the hands of someone who knows how to manipulate those doubts (such as the magicians of old), that demon, our weakness, the *Koach HaTumah* is a real force that stops our progress, dead.

From the rockiness we experience on the road to knowledge we know Hashem must have wanted us to struggle for knowledge. Once we have struggled we understand that only by solving problems do we develop our own powers of thought which make us God-like. But, so often on that road, the *Koach HaTumah* doubts described above make us despair of solving the problem with which we struggle. **In response to this concern as expressed by Rashi, Ramban and Chinuch, Parsha Shmini reminds us we have better tools in the Torah.** Tread the path of knowledge in the company of those who know Torah well – they will deflect the *Koach HaTumah* and help you find your life-changer.

In summary, Rambam emphasized the **ultimate futility** of turning to magic, Rashi et al emphasized the **present danger** of turning to magic. According to this interpretation of Rashi et al, people never flew on broomsticks and ghosts never counselled the living. Magic was never real vis a vis the reality of Hashem but was always real vis a vis our own ignorance. People were markedly influenced by the images of broomstick flying and ghosts as if they really did happen. Today, people are profoundly affected by the magical promises of fad diets, get rich quick schemes, theatrical portrayals of the good life, and so on. These not only don't work, they distract from what does; they are *Koach HaTumah* forces that are evil and dangerous. **For us, the last word on the subject has to be heard from both Rambam and Rashi et al because they both apply**.

אמור – Emor

Say

17 Masoretic Paragraphs, 124 verses;
Leviticus Chapters 21 - 24

Parsha 8: Seize the Day, Don't Curse It

The end of אמור is full of intrigue. Not only does it contain the infamous "eye for an eye" passage - "infamous" would be a better word for all the misunderstanding it has caused - but also the inexplicable story of the *m'gadef/*blasphemer (Lev. 24:10-23), the one who cursed Gd's name. So many questions arise about this *m'gadef/*blasphemer story.

First, why was he put to death? Rashi says that he was placed in a special holding cell because the court did not know what to do with him; they didn't even know if this was a capital crime. But, if the court didn't know, how could he have known, and if he didn't know, how could he be punished? The Torah only prescribes execution for wilful sins.

Second, why was he put in prison in the first place? If we hadn't been told of this crime yet, what would have prompted the court to even bother with him?

68

Third, why is the famous passage of "an eye for an eye and a tooth for a tooth" (Lev. 24:20), which details financial damages, placed right in the middle of the story?

And **fourth**, given what Hashem had just done for the Jewish people, how could a person in his "right mind" blaspheme and curse Hashem?

Rashi might be addressing this last question. The story begins by reporting **"the *m'gadef* went out"** (Lev. 24:10) but it doesn't say from where. Rashi quotes three opinions about the meaning of "he went out".

1. R. Levi explains he went out of his world. This is apparently a reference to the fact that he subjected himself to capital punishment.

2. R. Brachya interprets "he went out" as a rejection of the preceding parsha that described the *Lechem-HaPanim*/Show- Bread service of replacing weekly the twelve loaves on the Table. This man rejected the details of that service by scoffing, "A king of flesh and blood eats fresh bread every day, shall the Almighty eat stale bread for seven days?"

3. A *Masnisa* also interprets "he went out" as a rejection in reference, but in reference to a court decision. This man tried to establish himself within the Tribe of Dan but was evicted because only his mother was from Dan, not his Egyptian father. He took the case to court and lost. Angered by his defeat, he cursed Hashem as he came out of court.

I am surprised Rashi quoted all three interpretations of "he went out". We must realize that the stories told by R. Brachya and the *Masnisa* are not made up. **One doesn't make up such stories.** Therefore, why did Rashi quote anything other than the last story? It keeps the literal meaning of "going out" - from a place, the court - and presents the most likely scenario - that he felt so frustrated by the court decision that he cursed Hashem?

In order to answer, we need to examine the story more closely. Why did Dan evict him from their tribal camp? After all, his mother was from Dan and his father was an Egyptian so where else should he go? Were they so petty as to hide behind a technicality that everybody had to camp by their father's household? The answer is that they rejected him because **he was an outcast based on his own behaviour**. As R. Brachya reveals, he mocked the *Lechem HaPanim* service of the Mishkan.

Remember, the Jewish people were so devoted to the *Mishkan*/Tabernacle that they donated all their wealth to its construction and had to be restrained from giving any more. The hallmark of *Mishkan* service was unquestioned obedience to the rules laid down by Moshe. There was no rhyme or reason other than the revelation provided by Moshe. **This man who scoffed put himself in opposition to everything that the nation stood for**. Not satisfied with that he goes to court and sets himself up as the "official opposition". Upon losing, he doesn't accept the verdict of the court headed by Moshe, whom everyone reveres as the proven agent of

Hashem. Instead, he curses Hashem whose presence dwells in the midst of the people in the form of the pillar of cloud. He has now defied everything that everybody stands for – he has made himself a total outcast!

We can now understand why Rashi included all three explanations of "he went out". R. Levi's comment that he took himself out of his world was not a reference to his ultimate punishment but to the nature of his behaviour which removed him from the very context of his life. **Today, we might call it a hate crime**. Warnings against such behaviour would have been superfluous. The whole demeanour of the man was in such opposition to everything for which the nation stood that the question may have been; could this man still be entitled to the atonement that would come with a capital punishment?

Then Rashi goes on to explain how that came to be, through his scoffing of the *Lechem HaPanim* service which led to social rejection by the Tribe of Dan which, in turn, led to the court case, his defeat and then his defiant curse.

The gut reaction towards such an outcast is often to smash him to bits. Many of us have experienced these types of emotions. The one who cheats us deserves to lose everything; the one who harms us deserves to die.

Therefore, **the Torah interrupts our emotional reaction** by pausing the story to tell us this is not the way of justice. The reaction has to be measured. Before "an eye for an eye" it says "if a man kills another person, he shall be put to death". This emphasizes, only for a life do we take a life, but for an eye we take (the value of) an eye, not two eyes and certainly not a life, as we might wish.

One last question. The analysis above showed how the whole story started with his wicked criticism of the *Lechem HaPanim* service. Why was his criticism of the *Lechem HaPanim* service considered wicked? It actually describes a righteous indignation on behalf of Hashem – shall the King of Kings be given stale bread? **Why didn't they give him the benefit of the doubt?**

Since R. Brachya backtracks us to the *Lechem HaPanim* paragraph that precedes the story, let's do the same - backtrack to the paragraph before that, the one describing the daily lighting of the *Menorah*. **Why was there a different frequency between the two?** The *Menorah* service was daily but the *Lechem HaPanim* service was weekly. We could have provided bread daily and we could have lit the *Menorah* with enough oil to last a week. Furthermore, just as the *Menorah* signified the light of the Torah, the Table and *Lechem HaPanim* symbolized *Parnassah*/material-wealth. Why was *Lechem HaPanim* specifically replaced every week on Sabbath, the very day we are forbidden from pursuing *Parnassa*?

The answer lies in the reason for the symbolism. It is to teach us how to achieve the most success humanly possible. For most humans, success is defined by the number of possessions. As soon as they learn enough about themselves and how the world works, they figure they know enough about how to make *Parnassa* and thereafter strive after higher and higher *Parnassa* goals; they never have enough.

The *Mikdash* juxtaposition of the Menorah and its lamps opposite the Table and its *Lechem HaPanim* teaches us there are two fields of endeavor. **To reach success in Torah, it requires a daily effort**; that is what the daily lighting of the *Menorah* teaches us. We never know enough.

To reach success in *Parnassa*, it doesn't necessarily take daily effort. We attend work every day in the hope of success but individual days often testify to the cyclical nature of business. Some days, many days, it doesn't pay to show up. However, one never knows which days will pay, so we show up as often as we can. From this, our own experience teaches us we need Divine assistance. Moshe's instructions for the *Mishkan-Avoda*/Tabernacle-Service pinpoint this for us. **Success in Parnassa will depend on how we do on Sabbath**. If we fill Sabbath with *Avoda*/Service, then *Parnassa* will follow well enough to allow for more important pursuits.

The *m'gadef* understood this symbolism and rebelled against it. He preferred relying on his daily efforts to sustain him rather than recognize the Divine hand in *Parnassa*. This led to his downfall. The end of the parsha makes us reflect on this because many of us are tempted the same way. We would prefer to convince ourselves that we are self-sufficient rather than acknowledge we need help, even if it is from the Almighty, Himself. **But, at the end of the day, isn't it better to seize the help?**

בהר – BeHar

On the Mountain

7 Masoretic Paragraphs, 57 verses;
Leviticus Chapters 25 - 26:2

Parsha 9: Seen Hashem Lately?

The last verse of בהר provides the reader with a subliminal tug and an outrageously unbelievable claim. Subliminally, the reader wonders "Haven't I seen this somewhere before?" Then, thumbing backwards through the pages, "Yes, I knew I saw it before, just two weeks ago in Kedoshim, the exact same verse!" The words are, **"My Shabbats you shall observe and my Sanctuary shall you revere – I am Hashem"** (Lev. 19:30 and 26:2). Identifying for the reader the previous identical verse that tugged subliminally was easy to do. Demonstrating that there was a claim that is outrageously unbelievable will take a few steps, as follows.

First ask, why did the Torah set up the tug? There are many phrases repeated in the Torah but it is unusual to have an entire verse repeated word for word. We can at least explain the repeated warning about Shabbat. Perhaps, it is meant about the recently introduced Shabbats of *Shmittah* and *Yovel*. A new advisory warning is completely justified considering the extreme *Bitachon*/Trust In Hashem needed to desist from farming the entire year of *Shmittah* and *Yovel*. **But why repeat the instruction about revering the Sanctuary?**

In Kedoshim, two parshas ago where the verse first appeared, Rashi explained that Shabbat and Sanctuary were coupled together to teach us not to violate the weekly Shabbat even when doing something as exalted as building the Sanctuary. We cannot apply that teaching here because there would be no problem building the Sanctuary during a *Shmittah* or *Yovel* year – only farming is prohibited.

Rashi here does not address the coupling of Shabbat and Sanctuary although he does offer **a reason for repeating Shabbat.** For the last ten verses the Torah has been delineating the rules by which a Jewish government may allow a non-Jew to enslave a fellow Jew (temporarily, not permanently, because the Jewish people are ultimately owned by Hashem). Then it says, "you shall not make idols for yourselves, nor shall you erect for yourselves an idol or pillar, nor in your land may you emplace a flooring stone for prostration purposes, I am Hashem, your Lord" (Lev. 26:1). Rashi treats this as a continued comment on the instance of a Jew living under the rule of a non-Jew, "don't say that since my master the non-Jew acts immorally, worships idols, desecrates the Shabbat and the like, so too will I do – that is why these admonitions appear here".

Rashi mentions desecrating the Shabbat but not the Sanctuary, probably because the Sanctuary would not fit in. Under a Jewish government, we would never allow the non-Jew to desecrate the Sanctuary so the Jewish slave would never be enticed to do the same. More pointedly, even if the non-Jew did somehow desecrate the Sanctuary, why would the Jewish slave want to do the same? The sins of acting immorally and violating Shabbat have their attractions, but desecrating the Sanctuary doesn't.

An interesting approach can be found in the commentary of Sforno. Although Rashi did not explain why the Sanctuary was included, Sforno does by building on Rashi. Sforno applies Rashi's warning of not mimicking a non-Jew to a time when, not one Jew is enslaved, but all Jews are in exile and, thereby, enslaved by foreign influences. In such a situation, it is paramount for the Jew to preserve his holy times, such as Shabbat, and his holy places, such as the mini-Sanctuaries of prayer and study halls, in order to remember "I am Hashem". And why remember that? Sforno defers to Rashi who comments, "trusted to grant reward", implying, "for continued devotion even in trying times, one can be assured of reward".

This is the outrageously unbelievable claim mentioned earlier! Of what kind of reward are we assured? If it is the kind that occurs in the World to Come, why bother mentioning it? A final reward after death is a basic tenet of any religion. It does not have to be repeated each time. Instead, the assurance must regard a reward in this world! But isn't that unbelievable? Didn't even Moshe pray to understand why the righteous suffer in this world? If he couldn't see the reward, we certainly won't and if we can't see it, there is no incentive. In fact, if we can't see it then it doesn't exist in this world! The only reward we work for is the one we hope to get after death.

The insight that will solve all this comes from another unbelievable claim made earlier in the parsha. Those who keep *Shmittah* were assured they would have enough food till they planted and harvested again; Hashem will command His blessing to do so (Lev. 25:21). **What!?** Does this mean if the harvest is not enough for the next two or three years, I am exempt from *Shmittah* and *Yovel* because Hashem hasn't kept His part of the bargain? What about when He does keep His part of the bargain? If the harvest is super large, why bother commanding me? Common sense would dictate, "Hey! We have more than enough. Let's take some time off!"

In truth, though, Rashi saw all these questions coming and precluded them in advance. On "you will eat your fill" (Lev. 25:19) Rashi expounds **"the blessing will be inside you"**, i.e., don't expect open miracles. If, in a normal year, one truckload is gathered, we shouldn't expect three truckloads in the sixth year. That would be an open miracle. Rather, a little will go a long way, one won't be so hungry, less will rot or be wasted, or the food will just seem to fill one up faster; Hashem will look after things in a quiet way.

Since the Torah reveals this, it must want us to know this; to recognize when Hashem looks after things in a quiet way. The Lubavitch Rebbe, R. M. Schneerson, said on Rashi here, it is the wise son who seeks to discover how this works. For example, I remember once hearing that, **in the early days of**

the State of Israel, medical teams were sent to religious Kibbutz's that were keeping *Shmittah* and so were not expected to have a good supply of fresh produce. The intention of the non-religious agency was to show the "backward thinking fanatics" the harm they were causing their children's health by keeping *Shmittah*. Instead, the exams proved that the children in the religious Kibbutz's were as healthy, if not healthier, than their non-religious neighbours who were farming the land without regard to *Shmittah*.

In truth, the whole phenomenon of the modern State of Israel can only be explained by Hashem working in the background. Not only has it survived amid a sea of hatred and aggression from the entire surrounding region, the state has produced unmatched achievements in its 70 years. And no one can reasonably explain how. **A recent experience provided a poignant talking point.** On a tour of Israel a member of the group was a young American woman who had recently made aliyah. Being a CPA, she had secured a position with the Israeli arm of Price Waterhouse, an international accounting firm. Being a CPA myself, I took this opportunity to learn some financial facts about Israel. I asked about the cost of living, the tax rates and the average income. Comparing the answers I got regarding the modest average incomes with the number of cars on the road and the number of people in the restaurants, the numbers didn't add up. So I asked, "how does the average worker get through the month?" This CPA from one of the most prestigious accounting firms in the world who specialize in these kinds of analyses provided an unforgettable answer, **"We don't know."** I challenge the reader to come up with a better answer. All these are good examples of the quiet protection of Hashem, but I don't have the scientific data or documents to back it up. However, I did discover my own evidence of a this-world reward that deserves publicizing.

In 2002, Hashem's protection seemed absent because of the Intifada and the terrible headlines of terrorist bombs and sniper shootings that pictured Israel as the least safe place in the world. I decided to find out how bad it was and I made an amazing discovery – Israel was one of the safest places in the world!

The Death Rate of a country is the number of people out of 1,000 who died that year for any reason. From the statistics of the World Book of the CIA, I learned that the Death Rate in Israel for the year 2002 was significantly lower than many of the other countries people tend to visit. This remains true today – look it up: https://www.cia.gov/library/publications/the-world-factbook. Here is a summary of my findings.

Country	Death rate 2002	Death rate 2014
Israel	6.21	5.54
Canada	7.54	8.31
United States	8.70	8.15
United Kingdom	10.30	9.34
France	9.04	9.06
Spain	9.22	9.00
Greece	9.79	11.00
Italy	10.13	10.10

Full Disclosure: This may not be meaningful. After discovering this, I shared it again and again over 15 years without encountering an opposing interpretation, until I shared it with my friend Chaim Belisowski. He pointed out that the CIA also reports a relatively low average age for Israel. This could explain the lower death rate without relying on Hashem's hidden protection. The lower death rate might still be meaningful if there was a low correlation between it and the average age but I don't have the skills to determine that. Whatever the ultimate finding, the next paragraphs provide compelling insights into Hashem's hidden hand.

Here is another example of Hashem's protection occurring in advance. A demographics expert explained in an interview on Israeli TV (https://www.youtube.com/watch?v=Ra879tN9pAA 8 mins. Hebrew, subtitled) that Israel now enjoys an astonishingly high birth rate. This is true for many sectors of Israeli society. Even secular Sabras have the high birth rate of 3.4. The highest birth rate occurs in Judea and Samaria (West Bank) where it is 6! In contrast, surrounding Arab areas (including Palestinians and Israeli Arabs) are experiencing birth rates that are <u>negative</u> (below replacement). He concluded that **Israel has no need to fear being overwhelmed by Arab population growth**. On the contrary, there is every reason, demographically, to press for control over more land to accommodate an exploding population over the next two decades.

The last paragraph of the parsha (Lev. 25:47-26:2) speaks about resisting foreign influences. In "Under The Influence: California's Intoxicating Spiritual and Cultural Impact on

America" Monica Ganas demonstrates how California exerts undue influence on western society. This probably happens through the entertainment industry which is based there. Whatever ideas take root in California become part of the thinking of the entertainers living there who then spread those ideas far and wide through their work and public acclaim. California reports a birth rate of 1, one of the lowest in the world. When surveyed as to why they don't have more children, Californians responded **"self-fulfillment" – children are too expensive and time-consuming to allow the parents to fulfill their self interests.**

In a contrast that could not be sharper, when asked what prompted them to have so many children that results in 3.4 family growth, <u>secular</u> Israelis responded with the very same words, **"self-fulfillment" - children are the most joy, the fullest challenge and the guarantee of a future in which to invest**. I interpret their response as a natural outgrowth of influences that are <u>non-foreign</u> but rather the Torah lifestyles of the religious sectors in Israel. "I am Hashem" means "I am Eternal, I am always there" – we can rely on the ever present protection of Hashem.

So **the outrageously unbelievable claim mentioned earlier has been rendered believable.** We do receive reward in this world and, like Moshe, we don't see it. But we receive the benefits and those benefits allow us to continue on the proper path. Our incentive does not come from the promise of a reward because we are never able to trace the reward back to our behaviour, Instead, our incentive comes from our convictions in the wisdom of God's instructions. The reward is there, not as an incentive, but as an enabler that facilitates reaching our goals. That is the end we want.

בחקתי – Bechukosei

In My Decrees

5 Masoretic Paragraphs, 78 verses;
Leviticus Chapters 26:3 - 27:34(end)

Parsha 10: Received at Sinai

Was the last verse of בחקתי known to Rashi? Of course it was! Then why did Rashi contradict it?

Our last verse says, "These are the commandments that Hashem commanded Moshe to the Children of Israel on Mount Sinai" (Lev.27:34). The phrase "these are the commandments" suggests "these" and not others - **only the mitzvahs described up to here were given at Sinai**. This seems to contradict the famous Rashi at the beginning of BeHar which claimed all 613 mitzvahs were given at Sinai. Some *gematria* expert may try to amuse us by noting that the number of mitzvahs counted by the Chinuch up to here is 361, a number with the same digits as Rashi's 613. Everyone can grin appreciatively - but factually the contradiction persists.

Rashi's lack of any comment on this last verse indicates he saw no contradiction with what he said before. This suggests **the solution is obvious**, although it took me awhile to finally find the answer. It is in plain view in the phrase "to the Children of Israel" found in our verse. Rashi in BeHar was describing the transmission to Moshe, our verse here is describing the transmission to the Jewish people. All 613 mitzvahs were given to Moshe at Sinai. Here, our verse is telling us that only the preceding 361 mitzvahs were given over to the Jewish people while they were at Sinai.

Even if this is correct, though, we must still ask why we need to know which mitzvahs were given to us at Sinai, as opposed to any other place? And, it is not even clear which ones they were because an earlier verse, at the end of the Tochacha/Admonition, seems to identify a different group. "These are the decrees and the ordinances and the teachings which Hashem gave, between Himself and the Children of Israel, at Mount Sinai, through Moshe" (Lev.26:46). Between this last verse of the Tochacha and the last verse of our parsha appears the chapter that describes the laws of Arachin (asset donations to the Temple treasury or to the Kohens).

Well, which is it? Was it all the mitzvahs described up to the Tochacha that were given at Sinai, and only them? Or was it the next chapter, the laws of Arachin, and only them? Or, if both, why repeat the statement with the claim "these" each time? Also, why it is important to know they were given at Sinai? **Can one answer solve these three questions?**

R. Shimshon R. Hirsch addresses these last questions by focusing on the phrase "given by Hashem between Himself and the Children of Israel" found in the earlier Tochacha verse but not in the later Arachin verse. R. Hirsch contends the phrase implies a relationship, meaning that up to the end of the *Tochacha* are **all the rules that bond us to Hashem**; the rules governing *Arachin* in the following chapter do not contribute to that bond.

What kind of bond are we talking about? At Sinai we lingered for a full year (less ten days, see Rashi on Num. 10: 11) during which time we studied and exercised the mitzvahs we had received. This brought us to such a superior plane of existence we were able to build a *Mishkan* for Hashem's earthly abode. From the very fact that *Arachin* are completely voluntary, proves to R. Hirsch they are unnecessary to establish such a bond to Hashem. Not only unnecessary but also unable; R. Hirsch considers quite significant in this regard the absence of any mention of *Kappara*/Atonement or *Rai'ach-Noach*/Satisfying-Reaction from Hashem in conjunction with an *Arachin* pledge.

Our ability to be so close to Hashem that we could build a Mikdash was not optional; whatever brings us closer, Hashem insisted upon. Accordingly, we may gain additional insights into the power of certain mitzvahs by realizing they were included in the "short" list given to the Jews at Sinai.

So here we have **an answer for all three questions** asked earlier.

Question 1: Which group of mitzvahs were given at Sinai?
Answer: All the mitzvahs up the end of *Arachin* were indeed given at Sinai.
Question 2: Why was an earlier set identified by "these"?

Answer: Only the earlier set of mitzvahs listed up to the *Tochacha* bond us with Hashem.

Question 3: Why do we have to know they were all given at Sinai?

Answer: We have to know that even though voluntary *Arachin* were given at Sinai, they did not contribute to the higher level bond we experienced at Sinai and need not be indulged in the future.

The last point may be difficult to understand. **Why wouldn't a voluntary offering bring us closer to Hashem?** Doesn't this run counter to common practise wherein we voluntarily insert sincere, financial pledges in our prayers to show we care and hope that Hashem reciprocates by caring for us?

Perhaps, we should surmise that voluntary contributions do not enhance any connection to Hashem when they are directed to a Temple complex and its staff. The message would be that **it is too easy to assign to the Kohens the duty of relating to Hashem and allow ourselves to opt out.** That may be what R. Hirsch meant regarding the *Arachin* of Temple times.

In our day though, when donations are made to the poor, we do not expect them to be able to fill our role; we are just demonstrating our ability to emulate Hashem's mercy and kindness. We then hope that He will repay us in kind so that we will have an even better model of His mercy and kindness to follow next time. According to this line of thinking, membership donations to one's shul would not count unless one was donating more than his fair share which enables a less fortunate person to participate.

Summarizing the above, I have explained that Moshe indeed received all 613 mitzvahs at Sinai and, by the time they left Sinai, had taught us 361 of them. Those mitzvahs chosen to be the first ones learned were those that would be especially helpful in building a superlative relationship with Hashem. At the same time, a message was given through *Arachin* that the normal human expectation of reward for the sacrifice of assets was not to be the basis of our relationship to the Holy One.

Going back to Rashi in BeHar, why was it so important, in the first place, to maintain that Moshe received all 613 mitzvahs at Sinai? This question applies to both Rashi and his Talmudic source. "Tanya: **R. Yishmael** said, the general principles of the mitzvahs were told to Moshe at Sinai and the details later in the Ohel Moed. **R. Akiva** said both the general principles and the specific details were told to him at Sinai and were repeated in the Ohel Moed and then a third time on the Plains of Moav" (Zvachim 115b).

What is the issue R. Yishmael disputes with R. Akiva? Surely it cannot be where historically the mitzvahs were first said. What difference would that make? Also, how could R. Akiva claim that all the details were given at Sinai when Moshe did not know what to do with the request for inheritance from the daughters of Zelofchad (Num.27:1-7)? Perhaps that is why R. Yishmael disagreed with him.

But R. Yishmael's position is also difficult, perhaps, more so. Why would Hashem only give the general principles at Sinai and no details? What would Hashem have been implying? "I will eventually require you to keep Shabbat, Kosher and *Taharas-Mishpacha*/Family-Purity, etc....I'll tell you all about it later – over the next 30-40 years." **What should I do about it now?** Start making up my own rules in these areas!? Don't propose that R. Yishmael was describing an executive summary! They are provided to interest readers in the details that follow but the Jewish people have already expressed interest with *Na'aseh v'Nishma*. The efficient way to train is to start doing.

The above must be R. Akiva's reason for disagreeing with R. Yishmael. But then neither has answered the deficiencies of the other. **Why didn't they both use the simple meaning of the verse:** that just like the Jewish people, Moshe also only received the preceding (361) mitzvahs at Sinai – the rest came later?

I think the answer to all of the above requires an **appreciation for what it was like at Sinai.** Two parties had the experience, Moshe and the Jewish people. Hashem did not have the experience; He was the experience. Hashem being the experience means that no doubt was possible as to the authenticity and completeness of the experience – there is nothing like Hashem. The Torah is the name of that experience. To this day, **Torah is our window into an experience with Hashem** (although the window is much smaller or fogged up for us now).

R. Yishmael and R. Akiva agree on this fundamental principle, otherwise a part of Torah would be less authentic, less an integral part of the whole. R. Akiva would maintain that the experience did not contain the details – Moshe worked them out to his best understanding over his three time review – and this may be what the verse meant by "through Moshe". The implication is that authentic Torah might have been different had Moshe been more capable or less capable than he was. This may sound heretical but it is not; it simply acknowledges that **our Torah window into knowledge of infinite Hashem can never be totally accurate**.

R. Yishmael would maintain that even the details are dictated by Hashem – no variation was possible. It is all there. This too could be accused of bordering on heresy. How could infinite Hashem be defined by finite words? The answer would lie in the **infinite flexibility of how the words could be understood**. The implications of these two approaches are no doubt profound and beyond the scope of this work. I only seek to expose them for further consideration.

The last words of *VaYikra* echo the above. The experience of Sinai was described in *Sefer Shmos* using physical terms to describe what we perceived - thick cloud, thunderous noises, quaking mountain and so on. With the last verses of the *Tochacha* in our parsha, *Sefer VaYikra* describes Sinai from a spiritual perspective, starting as it does *VaYikra*, He called; then continuing with the *chukim, mishpatim, toros* and *mitzvos* with which He called to them, engaged them and empowered them - but not perfecting them. Even at the end of that unique time at Sinai, *beHar Sinai,* or perhaps especially at the end of that unique time, we realized that, consistent with the infinity of Hashem, there will never be an end to our spiritual growth.

Printed in Great Britain
by Amazon

58376087R00054